Russian Blue Cats

as Pets

ABOUT THE AUTHOR

"Karola Brecht is a publisher and writer living and working in Heidelberg, Germany. Miss Brecht is born and raised on a farm. When she's not reminiscing about her special friendships with Twinkle Toes, Emir and Blinky, she is working at a veterinary practice. She enjoys working with animals, especially with pets. If you want to leave her a message, please contact her at:

www.storie-di-karola.com

karola.brecht@storie-di-karola.com

She is happy about any message!

Russian Blue Cats as Pets

THE COMPLETE OWNER'S GUIDE-
RUSSIAN BLUE CATS PERSONALITY, CARE,
HABITAT, FOOD, SHEDDING, FEEDING, DIET,
DISEASES, PRICE, COSTS, NAMES AND LOVE-
LY PICTURES

Karola Brecht

Official Website: WWW.RUSSIAN-BLUE-CATS.COM

Storie di Karola – Waltraud Karola Brecht
Nussloch, Germany

Storie di Karola – Internet Marketing Business
Waltraud Karola Brecht
Siedlerstr. 11
Nussloch, Germany 69226
www.storie-di-karola.com
www.russian-blue-cats.com

Book Layout ©2013 BookDesignTemplates.com

Ordering Information:
Quantity sales. Special discounts are available on quantity purchases by corporations, associations, and others. For details, contact Karola Brecht at the address above.

Russian Blue Cats as Pets/ Karola Brecht. —1st ed.
ISBN 978-3-944701-04-2

CONTENTS

i

Acknowledgements

Thank you to Markus, my lovely son, who stuck with me through seemingly endless hours of research and writing.

Dedicated to my Russian Blue cat called Emir (in Arabic it's "Prince") - the most wonderful cat I've ever had. My heart is yours.

Also dedicated to the many feline icons throughout cartoon history who have been unfairly misrepresented including: Tom, Stimpy, and Scratchy.

FOREWORD

"Thousands of years ago, cats were worshipped as Gods. They have never forgotten this."

Of course this famous cat quote rings true for all cat owners - but is perhaps most apropos to this book's subject.

Folklore and history surrounding Russian Blues reveal many fantastic tales, putting these regal felines on the shoulders of Cossacks riding into battle and on the pillows of royalty.

And they weren't just any old pillows, but velveteen, down-filled feline thrones that resembled miniature clouds. (In the olden days, Russian Blues would accept nothing less lavish).

Given the Russian Blue's somewhat reticent nature around strangers (or "commoners," i.e. individuals outside of your family circle), it's obvious why these blue-gray beauties with their beguiling green eyes would pick the palace over the army camp. They were, indeed, favored cats of the Russian Czars and British Queens.

So... long story short. YOU, dear Reader, have a lot to live up to!

However, don't be distressed by this breed's privileged past. The Russian Blue is unusually empathetic with their human companions and will accept you as you are, regardless of your Royal status (or absence, thereof).

Owners insist Russian Blues are highly sensitive to their moods, and ever ready to offer comfort and companionship or to engage in a rousing and cheerful game of fetch. Special bonus: the cats are believed, in legend, to have healing powers. Of course, this remains to be proven and is outside the scope of this book.

Folklore also suggests that owning a Russian Blue is good luck, an assertion difficult to deny when you are the human singled out as the object of affection by one of these bright and intelligent cats with their sweet, smiling faces.

This book is ideal for Russian Blue enthusiasts as well as readers getting acquainted with the breed for the first time. The text will walk you through the rich history of this very "Royal Cat" and is chalked full of detailed physical and personality profiles of the breed, as well as practical information on; daily care, healthcare, breeding, and showing.

Also included are frequently asked questions, relevant websites, and even help naming your new pet. The glossary is filled with feline-specific terminology and a compendium of common plants that are toxic to cats.

If you are thinking of adopting a Russian Blue, this book will tell you everything you need to know about locating and working with a breeder — and bringing a healthy, energetic kitten into your life — a friend that, given the health of the breed, may well be with you for 15 to 20 years.

[1]

Introduction to Russian Blue Cats

{Please note that rates of exchange for currency conversions fluctuate. All prices cited in this book are approximations, and should be checked against the current rate of exchange.}

Russian Blues have been described as the "Doberman pinschers" of the cat world for their beautiful, muscular bodies, and also as cats that are best suited for "connoisseurs" because they are so thoroughly feline in their outlook and attitude.

These are not difficult cats with which to live, but they do demand attention from the human they pick as the object of their affection. They offer, for their part of the bargain, superior and intuitive companionship, making them one of the most popular of all domestic cat breeds.

ORIGIN OF THE RUSSIAN BLUE BREED

The elegant and aristocratic Russian Blue is believed to have originated in the port of Arkhangelsk on the White Sea just 150 miles south of the Arctic Circle.

Sleek and short-haired, these blue-gray cats are, according to legend, the descendants of the royal cats of the czars. Their plush coats, shimmering with silver highlights, developed as an adaptation to the cold climate of their Russian homeland.

In the 1860s, the cats reached Europe, likely aboard ocean-going vessels. Their first recorded appearance outside of Russia was in 1875 at the Crystal Palace in England. There, the breed was called the "Archangel Cat."

Initially, when Russian Blues competed in cat shows, they did so in a group with all other blue cats. In 1912, however, the breed was shifted to its own "Foreign Blue" class.

Breeding programs came to a halt during World War II. In the late 1940s, in an attempt to reinvigorate the breed, English cat fanciers outcrossed surviving Russian Blues to other blue cats including the British Shorthair, and even the blue point Siamese.

The goals were to keep the original Russian Blue's thick, pale coat, long legs, distinctive profile, and large ears.

Meanwhile, enthusiasts in Finland were also working to save the breed. Their efforts resulted in a different look, a line of dark blue cats with tight, short coats and glittering green eyes well placed in triangular heads.

MODERN RUSSIAN BLUES

Although Russian Blues were exported to North America in the 1900s, truly concerted breeding programs did not get underway until the post-World War II years. The Americans chose the finest examples of both the English and the Scandinavian lines, opting to breed out the Siamese traits.

The resulting "modern" Russian Blue is a fine-bodied feline with a dense, frosted coat. These cats have a robust constitution, an endearing personality, and a distinctive and sweet smile. Their expression is alert, inquisitive and open, with an active intelligence radiating from the depths of magnificent emerald eyes.

The Russian Blue breed has grown steadily in popularity since the 1960s. These are not your average gray cats, but a distinctive breed carefully cultivated not just for its unique appearance, but also for its outstanding disposition and highly companionable nature.

THE RUSSIAN BLUE AND OTHER BREEDS

Russian Blues were used in the initial development of the Havana Brown, and contributed to the creation of the Nebelung. In the case of the Havana Brown, which is the result of breeding Siamese and domestic black cats, there are no remaining genes from the Russian Blue in the breed today.

The Nebelung is still a rare breed and likely resulted from a gene mutation for coat length in a Russian Blue litter. Nebelung are semi-longhaired cats with blue-grey coats and green eyes. The first two cats to present with the longer coat were Siegfried and Brunhilde, born in 1984 and 1985 respectively. Genetic testing confirmed they were semi-longhaired Russian Blues, and they became the foundation cats for the new breed.

Often, Russian Blues are confused with British Blues. The latter however is not a distinct breed, but rather British Shorthairs that have blue coats.

The French Chartreux has a similar coat and coloration, but is a more burley cat and does not have the trademark green eyes of the Russian Blue.

The same is true of the Korat, which is a small to medium slate-gray cat with a heart-shaped head as opposed to the short wedge-shaped head of the Russian Blue, which is also rather long and flat with a straighter nose and longer forehead.

VARIETIES OF RUSSIAN BLUES

During the 1970s, an Australian breeder, Mavis Jones, crossed a Russian Blue with a white domestic cat to create the Russian White, a line with the same personality and physical characteristics of its blue-gray cousins.

In this same period, black Russian Blues were created by much the same process. Both black and white variations are accepted for show in Australia. They are exhibited under a separate class as "Russian cats." In North America, however, no other color variation of the breed is accepted.

THE DISTINCTLY "CAT-LIKE" RUSSIAN BLUE PERSONALITY

Russian Blues have been described as cats for the connoisseur of all things feline because they are so much the embodiment of all that makes the cat unique. Their natural instincts remain firmly intact, and they will "hunt" whatever prey is available to them, whether that be a catnip mouse or a hapless insect that dares to crawl across their floor.

My own cat thinks insects are the best toys ever, but the batteries run out entirely too quickly! What actually happens is that all the legs fall off, and then I step in -- literally -- and take over. What's funny is that he's so vigilant and dedicated to his "job" that he will return to the same spot repeatedly over the next couple of days just to make sure there are no more "invaders."

Part of the Russian Blue charm is their lively, playful nature. They will romp and wrestle well into their senior years. Timid around strangers and not receptive to rowdy children, a Russian Blue will simply remove himself from the situation, hiding so effectively he seems to have disappeared.

My cat seems to intuitively understand that he can totally disappear in a darkened room. He will close his eyes to become truly invisible and sit completely still. I've searched the same room three times calling his name and not seen him sitting under the shadows of a table more or less in plain sight.

That being said, because this is an inquisitive breed, they may eventually come out and have a look at strangers.

A Russian Blue will never be the kind of cat to just jump up in some random visitor's lap, but they may do a "drive by," allowing your guest to pet them in passing.

Russian Blues also have excellent memories. Once they have accepted someone, they will recognize that person the next time they come around.

The capacity both for curiosity and retention makes these cats great observers. Nothing escapes their attention. If you catch your Russian Blue staring into the corner or up at the ceiling, have a closer look; something is there. It may be nothing but a minuscule spider that you can't see without a magnifying glass, but your Russian Blue will spot it all the same.

I learned to trust my Russian Blue powers of observation the hard way. He was fixated on the space behind the refrigerator for days, and I kept assuring him there was nothing there and to move on.

Then I dropped my morning newspaper on the floor only to have it become instantly soaked with water that was seeping up through the wooden boards. My cat had been trying to tell me there was a leak behind the refrigerator, which he could see and I couldn't. I ignored him and paid the price.

The real mistake I made was in not understanding he was trying to speak specifically to me. Russian Blues make excellent family cats, but they will always single out one special person as the object of their complete devotion. That's me. My cat was requiring my attention, and I wasn't listening.

He may have muttered a little under his breath about having a slow human, but he forgave me. Russian Blues are wonderfully affectionate and they want open affection in return. The trade-off for the owner is absolute devotion, and incredible empathy and sensitivity.

I speak from personal experience. When I've had a bad day, my cat always knows, and he stays right beside me, often extending a paw and touching me as if he were patting my arm or shoulder comfortingly.

That great capacity for empathy is not without a lighter side, however. A Russian Blue always knows when to go for a laugh. They can be quite entertaining because of their rapt fascination with toys and their love of games, which often the cat will invent and "teach" to you.

I won't soon forget the day that beautiful little blue-gray ball of energy came bounding onto my bed, dropped a catnip mouse in front of me, and looked at me as if to say, "Do you know what to do with it?"

I threw the mouse, and to my great delight, the first of many games of fetch was underway. He'll go back and forth until he almost drops, and that can actually take a surprisingly long time.

All that grace and elegance hides an athletic and muscular body. These cats don't have a reputation as daredevils, but they get where they want to go, and are quite capable of some stunning jumps.

Overall, this is a tranquil breed. They are highly predictable cats, and they do not get aggressive. The stray hiss during a wrestling match is nothing but the feline equivalent of "trash talk."

This is especially true in litter mates that have never been separated, but even with other cats, Russian Blues are not bullies. They will take care of themselves, but they won't start anything.

The breed does not do well in large groups of cats, however. If there are many cats in the household and the Russian Blue is not getting enough attention, they can, like spoiled children, act out. Consequently, a Russian Blue does just fine as an only child, and will respond well to being one of a pair or even a trio, but more than that is pushing their level of tolerance.

PHYSICAL CHARACTERISTICS OF THE RUSSIAN BLUE

Russian Blues are typically very healthy cats with a lifespan of 15 to 20 years. Their bodies are lean and somewhat elongated with a dense, compact musculature. They average 8-15 lbs. (3.5 to 7 kg) in weight, with the males generally being larger.

COLOR AND COAT

As the name implies, the Russian Blue breed is especially well known for its short, bluish-gray, "double coat." The soft, downy undercoat is the same length as the upper guard hairs. These cats often look bigger than they actually are because their coats are so dense and plush.

The hairs stand out at a 45 degree angle, creating an unusually responsive thickness. It's possible to drag your finger through the coat and make patterns in the cat's fur. The "lines" you draw will stay there until you smooth them back out. The texture is as luxuriant as a seal's fur, and seems to

shimmer in the light thanks to the distinctive silver tips.

The overall tone of the fur is remarkably even, and seems to ripple over the cat's dense musculature. The light catches the Russian Blue's hair so perfectly, that the cat always seems to be highlighted to absolute perfection.

Some kittens are born with "ghost stripes," often seen on the tail and most clearly visible in direct light. All cats carry a tabby gene, even if it is not obviously expressed in their coloration. These stripes will fade as the Russian Blue kitten ages. If they do not, the individual will be considered pet quality, and not be a candidate for breeding stock or for exhibition.

Any white patches, or even stray white hairs will be seen as a fault in an adult and likewise disqualify the animal for breeding or show.

The blue-gray coloration is a dilute expression of the black gene. Dilute genes are recessive in nature. Each parent Russian Blue will have a set of two recessive genes, therefore Russian Blue parents always produce blue offspring. This means they "breed true."

The only other feline breed with a coat similar to that of the Russian Blue is the French Chartreux

THE EYES AND EARS OF THE RUSSIAN BLUE

Apart from its storied coat, the other major distinguishing physical characteristic of the Russian Blue are its eyes, which are a vivid green and alight with intelligence and interest. Yellow eyes in an adult Russian Blue are seen as a genetic fault, making a cat unsuitable for breeding or show.

A Russian Blue's eyes should be almond in shape, but are often mistaken for round because the breed opens its eyes wide when it is intrigued by something or is expressing anxiety about a situation. The eyes should be fairly wide placed and extremely expressive.

Many Russian Blue owners say they can have "conversations" with their cats simply by looking at the animal and readings its expression. The alert quality of the Russian Blue's face is highlighted by the distinctive eyes and enhanced by the large, broad-based and rather pointed ears.

[2]

Welcoming a Russian Blue Into Your Home

The decision to welcome a Russian Blue kitten into your life may mean you will be dealing with a registered cat breeder for the first time. You not only need to know what to expect from the cat itself, but how to locate a reputable cattery, pick a kitten, negotiate the adoption procedure, and bring your new pet into your home.

WHAT TO KNOW BEFORE YOU BUY A RUSSIAN BLUE

Russian Blues aren't just beautiful cats with sparkling emerald eyes. They're also highly intelligent and wonderfully playful. Although reticent around strangers, they are incredibly devoted to their humans to the point of being sensitive to and responsive to your moods. If you've had a bad day, your Russian Blue will be the first one to extend a kind paw and lend a sympathetic ear.

You can expect your Russian Blue to be there at the door waiting for you when you come in from a day at work, maybe with a toy at the ready for a nice game of fetch.

They enjoy looking out windows and commenting on what they see, engaging in that odd "clacking" sound cats often make when they spot a bird or squirrel. I've had my cat come and get me and ask me to follow him to the window so he can "show" me a new find. Usually a Russian Blue's voice is soft and melodic, but when they want to get your attention, they have no trouble speaking out.

At meal time, that same voice can be raised in a piteous wail complete with round and pleading eyes that can be very hard to ignore. Basically, Russian Blues are little beggars, doing their best to convince you they haven't eaten in days.

Don't fall for it! My guy had a regular little "beer gut" before I realized how much he was actually eating, and cut back on his food.

If you want to get a Russian Blue to disappear into thin air, show up with a rowdy child, or turn on the vacuum cleaner. It's disconcerting just how well a Russian Blue can evaporate. They will generally, however, come when you call their name, a fact that saves many owners the frantic search in fear their beloved pet has gotten out of the house.

With minimal grooming needs and a hardy constitution, these silver gray cats with their plush, dense coats are medium-sized cats with firm musculature and fine bones. They're beautiful to look at and beautiful to live with, which is why they are one of the most popular of all companion cat breeds.

WHERE TO BUY A RUSSIAN BLUE

Your primary concern in finding a Russian Blue breeder is to make certain you are dealing with a reputable cattery that has Russian Blue kittens for sale. Do not support the activities of backyard breeders or kitten mills. These animals are produced purely for profit, with no concern about genetic abnormalities or general health. They are often born into and raised in deplorable conditions with little if any socialization and no veterinarian care.

Many Russian Blue breeders do base their operations out of their homes, but they do so to be with their cats 24/7 and to provide all the care and attention these exceptional animals need. They do not engage in assembly-line breeding practices, they don't sell their kittens to pet stores, and they don't run ads in the newspaper.

They are passionately concerned about the welfare of their kittens, and will interview YOU to determine if you are an acceptable candidate to care for one of their babies.

You can locate lists of breeders from various feline publications and websites including, but not limited to:

- Your Cat at http://www.yourcat.co.uk/ (UK)

- Cats and Kittens at http://www.catsandkittens.com (US)

- Cat Channel at http://www.catchannel.com/classifieds/listing-russian-blue.aspx (US)

- Fanciers Breeder Referral List at http://www.breedlist.com/ (US)

It's always best to find Russian Blue cat breeders in your area so you can visit the cattery and meet the kittens. (See the section on Relevant Websites at the back of this book for some Russian Blue catteries online.)

WORKING WITH A BREEDER

Adopting a Russian Blue cat from a breeder is not a matter of looking at a litter of kittens, picking out a cute one, and heading home. Expect lots of paper work and lots of procedures. This simply means you are working with a high-quality cattery and a breeder who genuinely cares about his animals.

QUESTIONS TO ASK THE BREEDER

When you are in negotiations with the breeder, there are some important questions you will want to ask beyond the Russian Blue kittens price.

- Are the kitten's parents in good health and can you see certification of this fact?

- What diseases have they been vaccinated against and when?

- What conditions have they been evaluated for and when?

- Can you meet the kitten's parents?

- Has the kitten been dewormed?
- Has the baby received any other kind of veterinary care?

- How has the kitten been socialized? *

- Have any of the kittens in the litter been sick? **

- What forms of guarantee come with the adoption?

- Can the breeder provide references and can you speak with those individuals?

*Remember that Russian Blues are initially shy with strangers. It is not a bad sign if the baby is timid at first, but it should warm up to you and relax in a matter of minutes.
** If any of the kittens in the litter have been sick, reconsider adopting from the cattery. Many feline diseases are highly contagious.

How to Tell if a Russian Blue Kitten is Healthy

When you handle the kitten, it should have good muscle tone. The coat should be clean, with no thin or bald patches. Gently part the fur by blowing on it, and look for signs of dry or flaking skin.

Look into the baby's eyes. They should be bright, interested, and alert, with no discharge from the corners.

Also look for any evidence of nasal discharge, and make sure the kitten is not sniffling or sneezing.

Look into the cat's ears. They should be pink and clean, with no sign of debris.

Check behind the ears, low on the back above the tail, and at the base of the tail for signs of flea dirt, which will look like tiny specks of gravel or black sand.

EVALUATING THE KITTEN'S BEHAVIOR

Russian Blues are always a little stand-offish at first, and all kittens will naturally show caution toward strangers. After all, they're very tiny and you look enormous to them!

Within minutes, however, the kitten should become relaxed and interested in play. In fact, healthy kittens are little maniacs. They far prefer playing and getting into one adventure after another over being held and cuddled.

Bring a kitten-safe toy with you (not one with any small bits that can be swallowed) and see how the baby reacts. You should get a response that conveys alert interest. Don't bother with a toy containing catnip. A kitten has to be 6-9 months old before they are receptive to the lure of "nip."

MALE OR FEMALE RUSSIAN BLUE?

If you are wondering if adopting a male or female Russian Blue makes a difference in the cat's personality, don't worry about it. Both genders are gentle and affectionate cats. All breeders require adopted kittens to be spayed or neutered before six months of age so gender really isn't an issue.

AGREEMENT AND TERMS OF SALE

When you have selected a kitten, and are ready to move forward with the adoption, the next step involves a lot of paperwork. The purchase agreement that you will be required to sign will include some or all of the following information:

- breed
- color
- gender
- price
- name of the dam and sire
- seller's name and contact info
- buyer's name and contact info

There will also be highly specific terms of sale. These should reflect a genuine interest on the part of the breeder in the kitten's future life. If a contract doesn't include such statements, you may not be dealing with a quality cattery.

Some possible terms of sale might include:

- Buyer(s) agree to facilitate proper veterinary care for the cat/kitten, including yearly check-ups and vaccinations.

- Proper grooming should be provided to keep the cat/kitten happy, mat free, healthy, and clean.

- Without the written consent of the seller the cat/kitten will not be given away or resold for any reason.

- Under no circumstances shall this cat/kitten ever be given or sold to any research or testing facility, humane society, shelter, pet shop, or similar entities.

- If the buyer(s) can no longer care for this cat/kitten for any reason, the cat/kitten must be returned to the breeder provided the breeder agrees. There will be no refund or monetary compensation to the buyer(s).

- If the breeder does agree to the return, the cat/kitten must be tested by a licensed veterinarian and be negative for ringworm, FELV/FIV, and fecal parasites. The tests must have been performed during the previous week.

- all medical records and registration papers must be returned to the breeder, and ownership of the cat/kitten immediately reverts to the breeder. Buyer will assume responsibility for all applicable vet expenses.

These items are just an example of the kind of provisions that may be included in the terms of sale. All breeder contracts vary, and you will need to read the entire contract.

ADDITIONAL PROVISIONS INCLUDING SPAY AND NEUTER

Many breeders will also include provisions requiring that the cat be an indoor animal only, and not be de-clawed, which is widely considered inhumane.

It is common for the terms of sale to require spaying and neutering by six months of age, and the breeder will usually want to see proof that the procedure has been performed. In many cases the kittens offered for sale are pet quality, and the breeder is attempting to protect the integrity and quality of the blood line he produces.

HEALTH AND GENETIC DEFECT GUARANTEE

In exchange, there are some things that the seller should guarantee, primarily that the kitten is in good health at the time of the sale. This promise is usually accompanied by a requirement that the kitten be examined by a vet within 72 hours and a receipt of the visit provided so that the cat's health is verified.

(For the safety of other cats in your household, don't let them have contact with the new kitten until you are positive the baby is in good health. Many feline diseases are highly infectious and can be transferred by a simple nose tap.)

PREPARING YOUR HOME FOR A KITTEN

You will want to have everything ready for your kitten or new cat before they come to your house. Find out from the breeder what the cat is used to eating, and in what kinds of bowls. Do the same thing before buying a water dish. Try to keep everything as consistent as possible.

Discuss food with the breeder and get recommendations for how to progress through age-appropriate foods. Remember, the breeder works with show quality Russian Blues. Take their advice on proper nutrition.

You will want kitten safe toys that are free of any swallowing or choking hazards, a scratching post, and all necessary grooming tools. Russian Blues don't shed much, but their coats will benefit from routine brushing.

Start your kitten on a grooming routine as early as possible, and you'll have a pleasantly compliant cat on your hands. In fact, Russian Blues love the attention of their humans so much, your cat will probably ask to be groomed.

CAT PROOF THE HOUSE

Kittens are natural born daredevils and they don't have the ability to determine a good idea from a bad idea — they are completely driven by their curiosity, and firm conviction that they are just very, very small tigers.

Remove anything from the house that the kitten could swallow or get tangled in, including cords to all electronic equipment. Tape the wires to the baseboard or otherwise secure them, and cap any open outlets.

Secure or move any large or heavy objects that could be pulled down or tipped over. Install baby latches on cabinet doors, especially those where toxic household agents are stored.

Do everything you would do to "baby proof" a house and then do a little more. Russian Blues can be very determined about making a "discovery" when something has caught their eye.

HOUSE AND GARDEN PLANTS

Your kitten-proofing should also extend to plants, both inside and outside.

Many common household and garden plants are toxic to your cat. Lilies are among the most dangerous for felines, and poinsettias are the most mythologized.

The popular red holiday flowers will cause gastrointestinal distress in cats, but their toxicity level is considered mild. The real holiday danger comes from holly (the plant and the berries), Christmas trees, and all those miles and miles of electrical cords!

For a comprehensive list of plants that present a health hazard for your cat, see Appendix 2 - Plants That Are Toxic to Cats.

BRINGING YOUR KITTEN HOME

Follow all the breeder's instructions about bringing your new kitten home, especially if there are other cats in the household.

With Russian Blues, it's best to start them out in a room of their own for a few days. Put their food, water, and litter box in a quiet place and let them get used to the move and to you.

Let all introductions with other cats happen through closed doors. Cats can tell a lot about each other from sniffing and some cautionary paw play under a door. Make face-to-face introductions slowly and carefully. You want to supervise the interactions, but don't inject any tension into the situation. Cats are very good at reading your emotions and reacting to them.

Let the cats themselves decide on issues of territoriality and dominance. Obviously you have to protect young kittens from harm, but don't be surprised if it's your older cat that yelps and goes running off. Little kitten teeth and claws are very sharp!

Most kittens will acclimate on their own in 7 to 10 days and promptly start running the household.

THE INDOOR VS. OUTDOOR CONTROVERSY

Many breeders will require, as part of the adoption agreement that your Russian Blue be kept strictly indoors. In truth, given the dangers of the modern world, this is far safer for your cat.

In the case of the Russian Blue, there is the added factor of the cat's personality to consider. Since this breed is so wary of strangers, if they become lost, they are extremely difficult to find because their native caution is then overlaid with fear of the unknown. A lost Russian Blue tends to hide and will not respond to search efforts.

You can certainly give your cat time outdoors, but that time should be supervised and controlled. Contrary to popular perception, cats can be trained from an early age to wear harnesses and to "walk" on leashes.

This may be more a matter of you following the cat around while it investigates in your yard or garden than an actual organized stroll, but it's still more than enough to give your cat outside access while still keeping it safe from vehicles, dangerous dogs, bad humans, and a multitude of other dangers.

Apart from the fact that Russian Blue kittens are not inexpensive, the primary reason to keep a cat indoors is for its own safety.

THE APPROXIMATE COST OF ADOPTING A RUSSIAN BLUE

Typically a pet quality Russian Blue kitten will cost $400 (£264.55 / €305.50) to $700 (£462.96 / €534.63). Show quality kittens run $800 (£529.10 / €611.01) to $2000 (£1322.75 / €1527.52).

In terms of daily care, Russian blue kittens are no more expensive than any other short-haired breed.

Based on a life span of 15-20 years, and estimating $130 (£85.40 / €99.28) a month $1,565 (£1,028 / €1195.28) a year, a pet quality animal will cost from $23,475 (£15,421.76 / €17,929.34) to $31,300 (£20,562.34 / €23,902.2) over the course of its life.

(Beyond the Russian Blue cat price, these calculations don't include any unforeseeable major medical expenses.

Lifetime cost for show quality cats will be higher and include such factors as grooming, show entry fees, travel, lodging, membership, breed registration fees.)

Understanding Feline Body Language

Russian Blues, like all cats, use a complex body language to communicate. Unless a human has spent a great deal of time learning about cats, many of these subtle signals are completely misunderstood.

For instance, cats don't rub up against us as a sign of affection, or even a request for affection. They're making a clear statement, "This human is mine." By using the scent glands around their mouths, cats rub up against objects and humans to stake their territory.

If a cat really wants you to scratch his ears or pet him, he's much more likely to lean into you with his whole weight, or to simply insinuate himself in your lap.

Russian Blues are not pushy cats, but when they decide they want to be held, they will be held. They will also use head bumps to get your attention, and are also known to reach out with their paws and tap their humans lightly on the arm or face.

OTHER NON-VERBAL FELINE CLUES INCLUDE

Lifting and Shaking a Paw - That's "cat" for disgust. They don't like how something feels, smells, or tastes. Imagine the motion a cat uses when he steps in water. The message is clear. "I don't like this!"

Swishing or Lashing Tail - This one, humans usually do get right. Kitty is not happy. If his ears are upright, he's just annoyed. If his ears are back and his eyes are narrowed, leave him alone -- especially if he lets out with a hiss.

Tail Held Aloft - This is the ultimate expression of feline good humor. Think of that aloft tail like a flag that says, "All's well and I'm happy!"

Tail Held Straight Out - This is a sign of caution or wariness. The cat is still in a good mood, but they're reading the situation to see what's going on.

Tail Held Down - The cat is not happy, and is likely retreating out of the room. This can be an expression of fear, or simply an awareness that he's done something "wrong."

A cat might not apologize for turning over your house plant, but he will certainly understand he's done something you don't like and will remove himself from the situation.

While many non-verbal cues are universal in the cat world, don't lose sight of the fact that your Russian Blue is an individual. He will have his own vocabulary.

By watching and interacting with your cat, you will learn what he's trying to say. One of the fun things about this breed is that when they realize you're catching on, their natural instinct is to communicate even more so that in no time, you and your cat will have your own private language.

[3]

Daily Care of a Russian Blue

Russian Blues are actually very easy cats to care for on a daily basis. Other than a decided tendency to beg for food, they have the same basic needs as almost any short-haired breed.

MANAGING THE RUSSIAN BLUE'S DIET

When it comes to food, Russian Blues are absolute beggars. These normally quiet cats will turn into piteous panhandlers when they're trying to talk you out of more chow. They will eat whatever is put in front of them, which makes weight management high on an owner's list of responsibilities.

FEEDING SCHEDULE

Until your cat is 7 months old, feed him three times a day.

After that, twice a day, in the morning and early evening for life is a good schedule to keep your Russian Blue trim and healthy.

Don't let them free feed. These cats are very prone to weight gain. Get them on a schedule and keep them on it!

Amount to Feed

In consultation with the breeder from whom you purchased the cat and/or your veterinarian, select a high-quality dry food and give your cat .25 to .50 a cup U.S. (0.208 to 0.416 cup UK) per serving.

One small can (5.5 ounces / 14.17 grams) of high-quality wet food a day will actually help you to control your cat's weight since cats tend to gain more on a diet of dry food only. The wet food contains vital moisture, and it helps satisfy the animal's natural craving for meat.

Buying Your Cat's Food

Where you buy food for your Russian Blue is not nearly as important as what kind of food you buy. Traditionally, pet owners simply pick up cans and bags of food at the grocery store or market.

Large pet retail outlets generally offer the same products at reduced prices, and it's certainly possible to order in bulk online.

Should your cat ever need prescription food -- for instance to support a urinary condition, or as part of a weight reduction program -- you may have to purchase food at your veterinary clinic.

A high quality canned cat food in a twenty four count case (3 ounces / 85 grams per can) costs approximately $21.64 (£13.91 / €16.36).

This would be a twelve day supply. Sixteen pounds (7.25 kg) of comparable dry food is $24.25 (£15.59 / €18.33). The dry food should last a month.

UNDERSTANDING YOUR CAT'S NEED FOR PROTEIN

Cats are obligate carnivores, meaning that "by necessity" they have a biological need for meat. A cat cannot be a vegetarian, no matter how personally committed you may be to that lifestyle. It just won't work for your cat. He has a high animal protein requirement — twice as much per pound as dogs and humans. Growing kittens need even more protein than adult felines.

Cats also need fats, and if you read the label of commercial food, you'll see a great deal of fat in the ingredients. Cats don't, however, need carbohydrates to survive, even though lant-based carbohydrates are the largest component in many commercial cat foods.

This is one reason why it's essential not to skimp on your cat's diet. As a rule of thumb, the cheaper the food, the more it contains plant-based fillers.

It's also impossible to substitute dog food for your cat's nutritional needs, even though dog food may be cheaper. A cat cannot thrive on a diet of dog food, which does not have enough fat, protein, or the amino acid taurine, which is essential for feline health.

SELECTING APPROPRIATE CAT FOOD

Kittens do actually need kitten chow because it contains more fat and protein to support their rapid growth. Some foods, however, read "all life stages" and these mixes are also acceptable because they take into account the wide range of nutrients required for optimal feline health.

Do be aware that cats can be highly sensitive to texture. Some prefer pate or "smooth" wet food and others want chunky. There will be no mystery about this preference. If the food stays in the bowl all day and your cat is glaring at you, he doesn't like the menu!

FOOD BOWLS AND WHISKER STRESS

If your cat has a tendency to scatter his food, or to use his paw to pull his food out onto the floor, he may be suffering from whisker stress. A cat's whiskers, or vibrissae, are a type of hair that functions as tactile sensing organs.

Some cats don't like to eat in deep bowls because their whiskers drag on the edges and the cat finds the sensation uncomfortable.

Manufacturers of specialty cat products, like Wetnoz, produce anti-whisker stress food bowls that are more like gently curved trays in configuration. Most range in price from $25 to $30 (£16.42 - £19.70 / €19.09 - €22.90).

WATER IS A VITAL PART OF NUTRITION

Cats need clean fresh water at all times. A cat's body is almost 70 percent water, and water is essential to every one of its physical processes. You can encourage your cat to drink more by keeping its bowl clean, or by providing a source of running water, which some cats prefer.

This can be accomplished either by allowing a faucet to drip, or by purchasing a special water dish with a circulating fountain. These units retail for approximately $30 (£19.70 / €22.90).

HUMAN FOODS THAT ARE DANGEROUS FOR YOUR CAT

Given the voracious appetite of the Russian Blue, you do not want to get him started grazing on your plate. There are actually many human foods that are quite dangerous for cats to eat, so apart from weight considerations, it's not a good idea to share your meals with your cat.

Specific substances to avoid include, but are not limited to:

chocolate, coffee, anything with caffeine - Each of these substances contains methylxanthines from cacao seeds, an extract also present in some sodas. In cats, it causes a range or symptoms including vomiting and diarrhea, panting, excessive thirst and urination, hyperactivity, abnormal heart rhythm, tremors, seizures and potentially death. Dark chocolate and baker's chocolate are even more dangerous than the milk chocolate used in so many candy bars.

alcohol - Actual alcoholic beverages, as well as foods that contain alcohol cause vomiting, diarrhea, loss of coordination, depression of the central nervous system depression, labored breathing, tremors, abnormal blood acidity, coma, and potentially death.

avocado - All parts of the avocado contain persin. Avocado poisoning causes vomiting, diarrhea, congestion, labored breathing, and fluid accumulation around the heart. Avocados from Guatemala, which are the most common variety found in grocery stores are the most problematic.

grapes and raisins - The specific agent of the toxicity in grapes and raisins is not fully understood, but both can cause kidney failure in cats, especially those with pre-existing health problems that have weakened their systems.

yeast dough - When consumed, raw dough that contains yeast can rise in the stomach and digestive system causing painful gas and even ruptures. The risk diminishes once the bread is cooked, and a small bite as a treat is acceptable, although cats are rarely interested in bread.

raw or undercooked meat, eggs, and bones - The primary concern with raw meat and eggs is the same as it would be for humans. Both can contain harmful bacteria including Salmonella and E. coli. Additionally, raw eggs contain the enzyme avidin that decreases the absorption of the B vitamin biotin. This leads to skin and coat problems. Bones, especially chicken bones, are not only a choking hazard, but the bone splinters can puncture your pet's mouth, throat, stomach, and digestive tract.

xylitol - The sweetener xylitol is present in a wide variety of products and foods from toothpaste to baked goods. It can cause insulin release leading to liver failure. Initial signs of ingestion include vomiting, lethargy, and poor coordination. The poisoning progresses to a seizure phase, and liver failure can be seen within days.

onions, garlic, chives - Each of these items causes gastrointestinal distress and potential red blood cell damage in cats. An occasional low dose won't cause a problem, but regular consumption is a definite risk.

salt - Salty foods of any kind create excessive thirst and urination, which in turn creates a danger of dehydration. Symptoms include vomiting, diarrhea, depressed mood, body tremors, elevated temperature, and seizures.

"People Foods to Avoid Feeding Your Pets"
www.aspca.org/pet-care/poison-control/people-foods.aspx

"Chocolate Poisoning in Cats"
www.catchannel.com/news/november-06/2006-11-09-avocado-dangerous-to-cats.aspx

"Caffeine Poisoning in Dogs and Cats"
www.petpoisonhelpline.com/2011/09/is-caffeine-poisonous-to-dogs/

"How Harmful is Alcohol to Dogs and Cats?"
www.natural-wonder-pets.com/how-harmful-is-alcohol-to-dogs-and-cats.html

"Avocado Toxic to Cats,"
www.catchannel.com/news/november-06/2006-11-09-avocado-dangerous-to-cats.aspx

"Are Nuts Poisonous to Cats?"
www.pets.thenest.com/nuts-poisonous-cats-9245.html

"Grape / Raisin Toxicity in Dogs and Cats"
www.peteducation.com/article.cfm?c=2+1677&aid=2409

Common Sugar Substitute Xylitol Can Be Deadly for Pets
vetmedicine.about.com/od/toxicology/qt/xylitol_tox.htm

Is Salt in Cat Food Good or Bad?
www.pets.thenest.com/salt-cat-food-good-bad-10443.html

Many Cats Are Lactose Intolerant

"Cats drink milk," seems to be a matter of conventional wisdom. It is certainly true that cats LIKE milk, but most of us like things that are not necessarily good for us.
Cats don't produce large amounts of lactase, the enzyme that breaks down milk and milk-based products.

The result is diarrhea and an uncomfortable, upset stomach -- a fact you may not realize because all cats, regardless of breed, are very good at hiding pain. That's part of their survival instinct.

In The Cat: Its Behavior, Nutrition, and Health, professor Linda P. Chase of the University of Illinois College of Veterinary Medicine writes, "The only time animals are exposed to lactose is when they're babies -- in their mother's milk."

Lactose intolerance in cats is perfectly normal, and it increases in intensity as the animal ages. A kitten will tolerate milk better than a senior cat.

When a cat drinks milk, the undigested lactose passes into the intestine, drawing water with it where it intermixes with bacteria in a process that is basically fermentation.

Eight to 12 hours later, the cat may experience vomiting and diarrhea, or its stomach may simply hurt from the built up gases.

It is true that some cats can drink milk, but veterinarians recommend against it, saying the potential for problems outweighs any potential benefits.

Actually, for an adult animal, the only potential benefit of milk consumption is enjoyment, and there are much more appropriate treats -- for instance a bit of tuna -- than cow's milk.

Treats of any kind should make up no more than 5% to 10% of your cat's diet. The rest should come from high-quality, nutritionally complete food designed specifically for cats.

For more information see:

"Cats and Dairy: Get the Facts" by Wendy C. Fries
www.pets.webmd.com/cats/guide/cats-and-dairy-get-the-facts

"Dietary Reactions in Cats"
www.petmd.com/cat/conditions/digestive/c_ct_food_reactions_gastrointestinal#.Ua9QcfbF1Z8

"Lactose Intolerance in Cats"
www.petwave.com/Cats/Health/Lactose-Intolerance.aspx

"Is Milk Bad or Good for Cats?"
www.petside.com/article/milk-bad-cats

CREATING THE RIGHT ENVIRONMENT FOR YOUR CAT

Since it is strongly recommended that your Russian Blue be a strictly indoor cat, creating the right environment for your pet is essential.

LITTER BOXES

Russian Blues are exceptionally fastidious cats. They like their litter boxes to be cleaned daily, and are highly intolerant of odor and dampness. The breed is given to excessive digging, and vigorous covering behavior. You will want to select a covered litter box or an exceptionally deep pan to minimize scattering.

All cats have differing preferences for litter texture. As the breeder what the cat it used to, and purchase a similar product. Some cats do not like the rough texture of gravel, and do better with a sand-like clumping mixture.

For 28 lbs. (12.7 kg) of clumping litter, expect to pay $16.99 (£10.93 / €12.84). Ten pounds (4.53 kg) of gravel or non-clumping litter should be priced around $6.28(£4.04 / €4.74)

(Please note, that clumping litters cannot be flushed in a human toilet unless the box specifically says, "flushable.")

A covered litter box will cost approximately $20 (£12.86 / €15.12), with an uncovered pan going for around $8.99 (£5.78 / €6.79) Be consistent, and always buy your cat the same kind of litter and the same type of litter box. Russian Blues are not agreeable to sudden changes in the set-up of their litter boxes.

Window Perches

Russian Blues love to look out windows. They are great observers. If your cat could talk, he'd no doubt fill you in on everything that goes on in your neighborhood while you're at work. Window perches are a favorite of this breed. Commercial perches that combine a bed with a platform and bracing supports cost about $30 (£19.70 / €22.91). They install easily, generally fitting neatly over a window sill.

Scratching Posts

This breed also tends to be rather vigorous with its scratching habits. The practice of declawing has fallen from favor as an act of animal cruelty, and many adoption agreements specifically prohibit the surgery, which renders the cat essentially defenseless for life.

There are ways to discourage your Russian Blue from destroying your furniture while allowing him to hone his talons to his heart's content.

Herbal sprays like pennyroyal or orange essence ($12-$15 / £7.87-£9.84 / €9.16-€11.45) will drive a cat away from a piece of furniture. (Cats dislike both smells.)

Double-sided tape products ($8-$10 / £5.25-$6.56 / €6.11-€7.63) are also useful, since cats naturally dislike anything that feels tacky to their paws.

Take these countermeasures, and provide your pet with a scratching post, and you should be able to save your furniture. It's difficult to put a price range on scratching equipment, since some owners buy veritable indoor playgrounds for their cats.

A simple carpeted pole with a single perch could cost as little as $30 (£19.70 / €22.91) while an elaborate cat "tree" with multiple perches, stairs, and hiding areas can range from $100 (£65 / €76.38) to $300 (£196.96 / €229.14) and more.

HIDING PLACES

Russian Blues do need a place to hide. They are shy around strangers, and they will quietly remove themselves from any situation they don't like. This can be a disconcerting habit of the breed, since these cats can seem to just "disappear" — generally when you're just getting ready to leave the house and panic when you can't find them!

Your best bet in providing a hiding place for your Russian Blue is to let him pick one for himself. If it's a closet or under the bed, don't discourage his choice. At least you'll always know where to find him. Don't try to force your Russian Blue to come out until he's ready. Remember, these cats have a lot of native curiosity. Sooner or later, that will drive them out of hiding to check things out at a distance.

Toys

Russian Blues are a delightfully playful breed. They will happily occupy themselves with small toys like catnip mice, throwing them into the air and "killing" them on the way down. (A multi-pack of these mice, usually in lots of six, cost $5-$7 / £3.28-£4.59 / €3.81-€5.34).

Remember that these are highly social cats. They like their humans to get involved in games with them, especially those that involve chasing an object or leaping after it.

Wands that feature toys dangling from long string are an excellent choice for this type of play (and they keep you out of distance of the accidental paw swipe, claws extended.) Expect to pay $8-$10 (£5.25-£6.56 / €6.11-€7.63) for this type of toy.

Any toy that appeals to a Russian Blue's native curiosity will surely be a hit.

Any of these products (all of which are available on Amazon) would be great choices:

- Hagen Catit Design Senses Play Circuit - A multi-section hide and seek toy that gives cats access to a ball in a tunnel, which they can chase, but not remove from the toy.
The sections are detachable to allow for different configurations. - $10.95 / £7.01 / €8.26

- Bergan Turbo Scratch Cat Toy - Similar to the cat circuit in that it features a ball secured in a rolling track, this unit also incorporates a central scratching post. - $13.78 / £8.83 / €10.40

- SmartyKat CrackleChute Tunnel Cat Toy - A more elaborate take on the fascination of a simple paper sack, this cat tunnel is three feet long, so it can also serve as a hiding place. - $10.38 / £6.65 / €7.83

- FroliCat DART TR1 Automatic Rotating Laser Pet Toy - Complete with a timber and 16 combinations of movements and rotations, this automatic laser toy provides hours of fascination for your cat. - $27.99 / £17.93 / €21.13

Don't underestimate the fascination of a simple pack of foam balls, however.

One of the simplest of all toys, these feather-like balls will fly clean across a room, with your Russian Blue in hot pursuit. A pack of six on Amazon costs $5.75 / £3.68 / €4.34

Note that wand toys or anything with string is a "with supervision only" toy. String can be a choking hazard and can also cause serious intestinal blockages if swallowed.

GROOMING NEEDS

Russian Blues are clean to the point of fastidiousness and need very little grooming. They're so clean that if you pet your cat he'll immediately start bathing. This isn't a suggestion that you're dirty. Cats prefer to smell like "cat." He wants the attention, but he doesn't want your scent on his fur.

Although the Russian Blue's double coat is thick and plush, it sheds very little other than in the spring when all cats lose their heavy winter coat in anticipation of the coming warm months.

Your cat will enjoy being brushed and combed, however, and this will keep loose hair in his coat to a minimum. Baths are rarely required unless you're working with a show animal.

A good quality cat brush costs approximately $6.95 / £4.45 / €5.24, while a wire comb retails for about $10.75 / £6.88 / €8.11.

At an early age, teach your cat to allow you to clip his nails. This will help to cut down on the amount of destruction he can visit on your furniture. Be careful not to catch the vascular "quick" of the cat's claw. Not only is this painful for the animal, but the area will bleed profusely. Trim only the translucent tip of the claw.

Russian Blues tend to be "less restraint" animals. They don't like to be held down. If you start early with your cat on a routine of claw clipping, you should be able to hold the animal in your lap for the procedure. Take his paw in one hand and gently push downward to extend the claw. Clip quickly and confidently so you don't convey stress to the cat.

A good set of feline nail clippers sells for approximately $7 - $10 / £4.48 - £6.40 / €5.28 - €7.54.

Check your cat's ears periodically during the month.

You can normally do this when the cat has climbed into your lap for some attention. Sniff the ear to make sure there is no yeasty scent, which would indicate the presence of mites, and look for any black, tarry build-up.

Observe the cat's eyes for any sign of discharge. Cats are as prone to respiratory infections and colds as humans. A yellow to greenish discharge from the eyes or nose may mean it's time for a visit to the vet.

IS THE RUSSIAN BLUE HYPOALLERGENIC?

A Russian Blue cat is not actually hypoallergenic, but the breed does seem to be better tolerated by people who suffer from allergies. Russian Blues produce low levels of the glycoprotein Fel d 1, which lessens the histamine reaction in sensitive individuals.

Other cat breeds with low Fel d 1 levels include: Balinese, Oriental Shorthair, Javanese, Devon Rex, Cornish Rex, and Sphynx.

[4]

Russian Blue Health

The best news for prospective Russian Blue owners is that there are no genetic predispositions for specific illnesses in these cats. They are a naturally occurring breed and very healthy to the point of being robust.

WEIGHT MANAGEMENT IN RUSSIAN BLUES

The biggest problem you will face with your Russian Blue is his appetite. The breed will eat well beyond what it needs and never turn down seconds. Consequently, obesity and all the problems that go with it can be an issue unless you limit your cat's food intake, feed him on schedule, and ignore his begging.

(See Chapter 3 - Daily Care of a Russian Blue for more information on feline nutrition.)

A Russian Blue should fall in the weight range of 8-15 lbs (3.5 to 7 kg) in weight, with the males being larger.

To monitor your cat's weight at home, weigh yourself, then get back on the scale holding your cat, and do the math. Expect fluctuations of a half a pound or so up and down, but anything greater is a cause for concern.

Obesity can lead to a range of associated health conditions from chronic constipation, to liver failure, diabetes, hypertension, arthritis, and weight-related joint deterioration. Overweight cats cannot groom properly, and thus are prone to infectious skin diseases.

Without question, being overweight will shorten the life of your pet.

WHEN TO SPAY AND NEUTER

Consult with your veterinarian, but generally kittens as young as eight weeks can be spayed or neutered. If you have adopted your Russian Blue through a breeder, your terms of sale will include a preset period during which the animal must be altered, with proof being presented to the breeder.

You can also discuss the timing of the procedure with the breeder, since they will have extensive experience with the matter. The surgery should definitely been done before the cat reaches six months of age.

Costs for spaying and neutering vary widely by vet clinic. There are low cost options where the surgery can be performed for as little as $50 (£32.82 / €38.19), but you will want to ensure that the work is being done by a qualified veterinarian under safe conditions including the administration of anesthesia.

Since these procedures and vaccinations are the earliest medical procedures your cat will require, and many owners want established records with a vet, this is a good time to select a veterinarian with whom you will work throughout your cat's life.

You should consider the possibility that you may have to pay slightly more to establish this relationship. Most pet owners feel this is a necessary expense and do not mind paying extra for good, quality care.

VACCINATIONS

Although vaccinations have become controversial in both animals and humans in recent years, the procedure of "shots" for kittens and "boosters" for adult cats has immeasurably reduced the spread of contagious disease among cats.

There have, however, been reported incidents of cats developing tumors at the site of their vaccinations, leading some owners to be reluctant to agree to the injections.

Discuss the vaccination process thoroughly with your vet, and independently research the topic before making a decision. If you do decide to have your pet vaccinated, the recommended course of shots includes:

- Distemper combination*, begin at age 6 weeks and repeat every 3-4 weeks until 16 months, booster at 1 year, then every three years

- Feline leukemia, begin at age 8 weeks and repeat in 3-4 weeks, booster at 1 year, with annual boosters for cats at risk of exposure.

- Rabies, begin according to local law and type of vaccine used, then annually.

* This combination includes panleukopenia (FPV or feline infectious enteritis), rhinotracheitis (FVR is an upper respiratory or pulmonary infection), and calicivirus (causes respiratory infections), and can include Chlamydophilia (causes conjunctivitis).

On average, vaccinations cost $40 (£26.26 / €30.55) per shot although prices can vary widely.

PREVENTATIVE HEALTHCARE

A Russian Blue is a long-lived cat of 15 to 20 years. Although healthy by nature, it's your responsibility to actively monitor your cat's health and to take the necessary steps for sound preventive healthcare. This not only ensures that your pet is happy and well, but it will significantly reduce the chance that you will have to face major vet bills.

SIGNS OF POTENTIAL BAD HEALTH

Cats can be very secretive about how they're feeling so it's up to you to know your pet and to know what's normal and what's not.

Simply petting and interacting with your cat with an awareness of its overall physical condition is a vital part of this process. Look for:

- Any change in weight, gain or loss. Cats at a healthy weight have a normal pad of fat over the ribs. This pad should not, however, keep you from feeling the ribs if you press gently.

- A change in gait, including limping or a reluctance to jump onto surfaces normally accessed easily.

- A cat's nose should be moist and clean, not dry, cracked, irritated, or bleeding. There should be no sign of nasal discharge.

- Look for moist, bright eyes. The pupils should be perfectly centered and equal in size. The whites of the eyes should have no discoloration and only a few blood vessels visible. There should be no watering or discharge from the eyes.

- Make sure the ears are dry, clean, smooth, and without irritation. If a cat's ears are itching (usually from the presence of mites) the animal can wound itself scratching. There should be no odor, no internal swelling, and no internal debris. If the cat flinches when his ears are touched, it's time for a visit to the vet.

- A cat should have white, clean teeth with uniformly pink gums. Regular dental exams are essential, since mouth cancers do occur in all cat breeds. If you observe discolored gums, any sign of blood, or any lumps or bumps in or around your cat's mouth, immediately seek the advice of a veterinary professional.

- Check the capillary refill time of the cat by pressing against the gum with your finger and releasing it quickly. The gum's color will go white and then should return to pink in one to two seconds. This is a crude evaluation of how the animal's circulatory system and heart are functioning.

If you begin when the cat is young, it's perfectly possible to brush your cat's teeth, which gives you better access to monitor his dental health. You can obtain feline tooth brushes and tooth paste from your vet or at any big box pet store. Oral hygiene kits with everything you need generally cost $7-$10 (£4.60-£6.56 / €5.34-€7.63).

Watch your cat's breathing. It should be easy and emanate mainly from the chest, not the abdomen, which should barely move when the cat inhales and exhales.

Run your hands over your cat's body. Any masses, lumps, or bumps should be evaluated immediately.

To make sure your cat is not dehydrated, pull the skin just behind the shoulder blades up into a "tent" and let it go quickly. It should immediately pop back into its normal position. It resumes its normal shape slowly or remains tented, and if the gums are dry to the touch with a sunken appearance about the eyes, dehydration is present.

DON'T NEGLECT CHANGES IN BEHAVIOR

Even if your cat has no overt physical signs of illness, his behavior may betray the fact that something is not right. If a cat — especially a Russian Blue — goes a day without eating, be concerned.

Changes in litter box habits, including "missing" or going outside the box are often interpreted as behavioral issues, but may be a sign of sickness. If your cat tries to do its business inside the box and experiences pain, the cat's reaction is to not go back in the box.

The cause of the discomfort could be a urinary tract infection, a bladder blockage (common in altered males), a bowel blockage (which can result from the presence of very large hairballs), or even the onset of diabetes.

Drinking habits are also an important indicator. Cats drink more in the summer, but a cat that is suddenly very thirsty could be experiencing the symptoms of diabetes.

Remember that Russian Blues are very tidy cats. When your pet stops paying attention to his grooming, he doesn't feel well.

CHOOSING A VETERINARIAN

Russian Blues have no ongoing need for a specialist, and can be treated by any qualified small animal veterinarian. It is now common in larger urban areas for some practices to be dedicated exclusively to the treatment of felines.
If this is an option, it can be a decided advantage with a Russian Blue, helping to mitigate their nervousness and their natural reticence around strangers.

When transporting a cat to the vet, always secure the animal in a travel crate. Never open the door of the crate until you are safely in the exam room with the doors closed.

A good quality travel crate for your Russian Blue should cost from $30-$50 (£19.24-£32.07 / €22.66-€37.77)

It's important to have a good working rapport with your vet. You want to work with someone who clearly understands how much your pet means to you and who is willing to answer your questions and to point you to additional reference information and resources in the event of a major illness.

A "regular" visit to the vet for a checkup and routine exam costs approximately $50 to $75 (£32.04 to £48.06 / €37.74 to €56.61), but please be aware that these prices vary widely by practice.

[5]

Breeding and Showing Russian Blues

Dedicated cat breeders, regardless of the variety of feline with which they work, honestly admit they rarely turn a profit. Don't think about breeding Russian Blue cats for any other reason but love of the animals.

If you are extremely lucky, you'll break even financially. The real reward is in sharing a significant portion of your life with these beautiful creatures and knowing that you have contributed to the genetic strength and integrity of the breed.

For people with a competitive streak, breeding and showing Russian Blues can be a highly rewarding avocation, but do be warned. Russian Blues, for all their beauty, don't have a reputation for being cooperative show animals.

You will always have to be guided by the individual cat's personality, and some simply will not "take to the stage."

An Introduction to Breeding Russian Blues

Although prices vary, show quality Russian Blue kittens cost from $800 (£525.69 / €611.03) to $2000 (£1314.24 / €1527.59) depending on the bloodlines involved. That's just the start of a long line of expenses, including stud fees if you cannot afford a breeding pair.

Expect to pay anywhere from $600 (£459 / €458.22) to $2000 (£1314.24 / €1527.59) for stud services with additional charges for travel since the queen will have to board at the stud facility for several weeks.

Should you decide to keep a breeding pair of your own be prepared to physically alter your house. You will want to keep the animals separate to prevent unplanned litters of kittens. (This is especially crucial when your queen is in season.)

Other expenses include, but are not limited to:

- Regular and extraordinary vet bills.
- Food and litter multiplied by the number of cats you're keeping.
- Pregnancy related expenses including special nutrition and vet procedures.
- Vaccinations and health care for the kittens, plus their nutritional and housing needs.

Don't forget about fees for registrations, pedigrees, licenses if your city requires them, zoning permits, and showing costs if you exhibit your cats.

THE TIME COMMITMENT TO BREED CATS IS SIGNIFICANT

Russian Blues are fastidiously clean animals. The more cats you have, the more litter boxes to clean, the more stray cat hair to pick up, the more bowls to wash — and so on, and so on. The healthiest cats live in the cleanest conditions, so breeders are making a daily commitment to maintain the environment in which the cats live.

These cats make excellent mothers. The queens are loving and attentive with the kittens, but in that rare instance when a mother rejects her young, or has insufficient milk to feed the kittens, the babies will have to be hand fed every 2 to 3 hours — 24 hours a day — seven days a week — for five to six weeks.

(Note that the average size of a Russian Blue litter is three kittens.)

If you work, you will have to hire someone to do the feedings for you, and you certainly won't be getting much sleep until the babies are weaned.

Depending on the extent to which the mother might reject the kittens, you may also find yourself performing other maternal chores. For instance, mother cats lick their kittens not just to clean them, but to stimulate their breathing and their digestion. These could be chores you will have to perform as well.

GET TO KNOW OTHER BREEDERS FIRST

If you think you are interested in breeding Russian Blues, you should first get to know another breeder.

Learn about how their operation is set up, and find out exactly what is involved in caring for the cats.

Remember, you will be dealing with people who are passionate about the breed and devoted to furthering its genetic integrity and welfare. Listen to them and learn.

Never go into something as serious as breeding any kind of animal without learning all there is to know first, understanding the costs and other commitments involved, and making sure the endeavor is right for you. This is not just a matter of trouble and expense, the welfare of living creatures will be dependent on the decisions you make.

Considering the Emotional Cost of Breeding

For some people, the real cost that comes with breeding cats is emotional. Russian Blues are highly engaging, affectionate, and loving animals. Their kittens, with those vivid green eyes and big ears are, in a word precious. For many people, it's just too hard to raise the babies and then have to give them up.

There is also the apprehension that no matter how carefully the kittens are placed, they will not be cared for in a way that is up to your standards. You may be shocked at just how deeply you come to care about those babies.

If this is the case, you can certainly raise Russian Blues for your own pleasure, but you may want to confine your efforts to a single litter, with careful placement of the babies among your friends or family. These cats do fine as solo pets, but they aren't happy in big groups because they tend to start feeling neglected.

Typically, Russian Blues are not demanding cats, but they do single out people for their affections. If you're the only person at the beck and call of a gang of Russian Blues, you're going to get stretched thin fairly quickly, and the cats won't be happy.

INTERESTED IN SHOWING CATS?

NOTE: The following information attempts to provide a broad overview of the process involved in exhibiting cats at organized cat shows. I do not believe that this is a natural environment for a cat, especially a Russian Blue, and I strongly recommend against showing your cat. The stresses are far too great on the animal, especially this breed, which is not only highly intelligent, but subject to severe stress around strangers.

If you are interested in showing your Russian Blue, the point bears repeating — the breed does not have a great reputation as a show cat — not because they aren't beautiful and magnificent, but because they simply don't like the show atmosphere.

Before you make the decision, attend some cat shows first as a spectator to get a feel for the event with your cat's personality in mind. There is an entire "culture" around showing cats that can be hard for newcomers to comprehend without some preparation.

(Cat magazines, especially those put out by breed clubs, can be helpful in this regard.) Beyond that, however, a cat show has to be experienced in person to really understand the "vibe" that turns many Russian Blues "off" instantly.

The decision to show your cat really must lie with the cat. Russian Blues are so wary of strangers, that a show may simply be too stressful for the animal, especially if it's not fond of being handled and held.

You'll never have a successful show experience with a cat determined not to be shown, and, although not aggressive or difficult in general, Russian Blues can be incredibly stubborn when they're determined to have their way.

CAT SHOW ETIQUETTE

There are many unwritten rules for spectator behavior at cat shows that are extremely important, especially if you're trying to break into the culture. The most important of all is DO NOT TOUCH. You'll see plenty of signs to that effect, on practically every cage.

OBEY THEM. Bacteria and viruses spread very easily from cat to cat. If you pet an infected cat, those microorganisms transfer to your hands.

Exhibitors aren't being snobs when they tell you not to handle their animals. They're protecting them and every other cat in the hall. If you are invited to touch a cat, you are being paid a supreme compliment. Treat it with appropriate respect, and when you are asked to sanitize your hands — and you will be — comply politely and thoroughly.

The next most important rule is "right of way." Cat shows are crowded and busy. When competitors are called to the ring, they have only a very short amount of time to get there without being disqualified.

If someone yells, "right of way", MOVE. And don't be offended if you're talking to an exhibitor and they suddenly grab their cat and leave. They've been called to the ring and don't have the time to stop and explain.

If you are at a cat show and someone yells, "Loose cat," FREEZE. Do NOT try to help. Stand still, stay out of the way, and let the people who know the cat recapture it. Should you see the animal, it's fine to signal the location, but DO NOT HELP.

Finally, when you are in the vicinity of the judging ring, BE QUIET and STILL. This is serious business for the exhibitors. Don't do anything to distract them, the cats, or the judges. Besides, you'll learn a lot if you listen. Judges often explain to the spectators what they're seeing as they judge a cat according to the given breed standard.

How Do Cat Shows Work?

Cat shows tend to have a more quirky atmosphere than dog shows. Exhibitors decorate and customize their animals' cages, and overall the event is surprisingly noisy and hectic. Other key differences in cat and dog shows include:

- Cats stay in their cages when the judges are not evaluating them.

- Although hectic in atmosphere, the progress of cat shows is slower.

- There is a class for household pets.

- Cats are less receptive to being judged and often stage dramatic escapes.

Judging is performed according to breed standards established by the show's governing or sponsoring body. The more a cat conforms to the ideal features for the breed as set forth in the standard, the higher the score awarded.

At shows sponsored by The Cat Fanciers' Association, as an example, there are several shows going on at once in different rings, each overseen by a different judge.
Owners are given a cage number. When that number is called, the owner brings the cat to the specific ring, where judges handle and inspect the animal, determining a rating.

Rings are administered by ring clerks and ring stewards. These officials maintain the show records, call out the participants' numbers, and clean the cages between cats. A master clerk organizes all the records for the complete show.

The classes include:

- **Championship** - Intact cats of at least 8 months of age may compete.

- **Premiership** - Altered cats that would otherwise qualify for the championship class.

- **Provisional** - Cat breeds that are not yet fully recognized by the CFA.

- **Kittens** - Both intact and altered cats age 4-8 months.

- **Miscellaneous** - Breeds that have not yet achieved provisional status.

- **Veteran** - Cats that are age 7 years or older.

- **Household Pet** - Any cat that has not been declawed, has been altered, and is 8 months or older.

In specialty shows, cats compete against others of the same gender and coat color first. Ribbons awarded differ by group, but in the CFA they are:

- Blue - first
- Red - second
- Yellow - third

The first-place cat is also given a striped red, white, and blue winner's ribbon. After six such ribbons are accrued by a single cat, it earns the title "champion" and then competes against other champions. When a champion has earned 200 points, it advances to the title "grand champion."

In the premier class, a cat is named a "premier" when it has six winner's ribbons, and becomes a "grand premier" after earning 75 points.

Kittens do not get winner's ribbons and cannot compete for best-of-breed. Household pets are given red and white striped merit awards.

After the open class (all cats) has been judged, the champions and premiers are evaluated and can receive the following ribbons:

- Best-of-Color — black
- Second Best-of-Color — white

- Best-of-Breed — brown
- Second Best-of-Breed — orange
- Best Champion - purple
- Best Premier – Purple

In the last round of evaluation, the judge holds finals and gives out rosettes to ten favorite cats.

In major events like the CFA-Iams Cat Championship, a best in show award is also given out.

BREED STANDARDS

The Russian Blue is recognized by:

- The International Cat Association (TICA)
- Fédération Internationale Féline (FIFe)
- The Cat Fanciers' Association (CFA)
- Australian Cat Federation (ACF)
- The Governing Council of the Cat Fancy (GCCF)
- Canadian Cat Association (CCA)
- The American Association of Cat Enthusiasts (AACE)
- American Cat Fanciers Association (ACFA)

The Australian Cat Federation and The Governing Council of the Cat Fancy also recognize Russian Blues in white and black.

The American Cat Fanciers Association recognizes Russian Shorthairs in white, black and blue.

While each organization's breed standard may vary slightly, these are the major points of scoring as set forth by the The Cat Fanciers Association. A maximum 100 points are available in judging:

- Head and Neck, 20
- Body Type, 20
- Eye Shape, 5
- Ears, 5
- Coat, 20
- Color, 20
- Eye Color, 10

In general, judges are looking for show cats that are in good physical condition with a firm muscle tone and an alert, engaged air.

The following descriptions are taken from the CFA breed standard (at http://cfa.org/Portals/0/documents/breeds/standards/russian.pdf, as accessed in May 2013.)

Head: Smooth, medium wedge, neither long and tapering nor short and massive. Muzzle is blunt, and part of the total wedge, without exaggerated pinch or whisker break. The top of skull is long and flat in profile, gently descending to slightly above the eyes, and continuing at a slight downward angle in a straight line to the tip of the nose.

No nose break or stop. Length of top-head should be greater than length of nose. The face is broad across the eyes due to wide eye-set and thick fur.

Muzzle: Smooth, flowing wedge without prominent whisker pads or whisker pinches.

Ears: Rather large and wide at the base. Tips more pointed than rounded. The skin of the ears is thin and translucent, with little inside furnishing. The outside of the ear is scantily covered with short, very fine hair, with leather showing through. Set far apart, as much on the side as on the top of the head.

Eyes: Set wide apart. Aperture rounded in shape.

Neck: Long and slender, but appearing short due to thick fur and high placement of shoulder blades

Nose: Medium in length.

Chin: Perpendicular with the end of the nose and with level under-chin. Neither receding nor excessively massive.

Body: Fine boned, long, firm, and muscular; lithe and graceful in outline and carriage without being tubular in appearance.

Legs: Long and fine boned.

Paws: Small, slightly rounded. Toes: five in front and four behind.

Tail: Long, but in proportion to the body. Tapering from a moderately thick base.

Coat: Short, dense, fine, and plush. Double coat stands out from body due to density. It has a distinct soft and silky feel.

Disqualify: Kinked or abnormal tail. Locket or button. Incorrect number of toes. Any color other than blue. Long coat.

Color: Even bright blue throughout. Lighter shades of blue preferred. Guard hairs distinctly silver-tipped, giving the cat a silvery sheen or lustrous appearance.

A definite contrast should be noted between ground-color and tipping. Free from tabby markings. Nose leather: slate grey. Paw pads: lavender pink or mauve. Eye color: vivid green.

Afterword

For all the fanciful legends of Cossacks and czars, the real origin of the Russian Blue, like that of so many naturally occurring breeds, is shrouded in mystery.

There is no specific evidence that these cats originated in northern Russia, but by the same token, there's nothing to say they didn't.

Russian Blues themselves refuse to reveal their Royal secrets... and we've tried to get them to spill the beans here in our lab! Knowing how much Russian Blues enjoy feasting like Kings, we've tempted them with every delicacy, from oysters to caviar. But the regal creatures simply gaze out placidly from their royal pillows with their knowing green eyes and content little smiles.

Keen observers of the world around them, and especially of the humans they single out to be their special companions, these sleek and muscular cats have grown in popularity as prized companions since the 1960s.

They are not especially good show cats, disliking the hustle and bustle of the exhibit hall, but they are wonderful friends. A Russian Blue will greet you at the door at the end of the day, ready with a sympathetic paw to listen to tales of your awful day at the office.

Intelligent, curious, and a skilled problem solver, a Russian Blue quietly assumes the supervisory role in your house and life, but he does so pleasantly, and without being pushy. These cats are healthy and robust, some living to 20 years of age with no significant illnesses.

They do well with older, quieter children and will get along with other pets, but dislike being part of a large group. If you are a Russian Blue's chosen confidant, be prepared to be needed by your cat — and to give up your pillow. Russian Blues love to sleep with their Royal Family. Normally this breed is not in the least bit insistent (except at chow time), but don't think you'll get away with ignoring them either.

If a Russian Blue's personality and preferences fit you and your life, and you decide to move forward with an adoption, it won't be long before you realize the truly exceptional nature of the breed.

Distinctly "cat" in their ways and attitudes, the Russian Blue is indeed a companion for the feline connoisseur (and one that does not disappoint). So remove the crocodiles from the moat, lower the gates, have the guards stand down, and invite this Blue Emperor (and sometimes court jester) into your castle!

References

Davis, Karen Leigh. "The Everything Cat Book." Adams Media, 2006. http://books.google.com/books?id=J9ONFP1cJJsC&dq=everything+cat+book&source=gbs_summary_s&cad=0 (Accessed April 2013).

Eliot, T.S. "The Naming of Cats." Famous Poets and Poems, http://famouspoetsandpoems.com/poets/t__s__eliot/poems/15121 (Accessed January 2013).

"Frequently Asked Questions About Russian Blue Cats," The Russian Blue, http://www.russianblue.info/russian_blue_faqs.htm (Accessed March 2013).

Johnson, Margaret. "Breed Profile: Getting to Know the Russian Blue" in The Cat Fanciers Association Complete Cat Book as reprinted by Cats Center Stage, http://www.catscenterstage.com/breeds/russian-blue2.shtml (Accessed March 2013).

Longley, Ken and Pat. "What to Consider If You Think You'd Like to Become a Breeder." The Illuzion Cattery, http://www.icehouse.net/illuzion/want_breedup.html (Accessed April 2013).

McGrath, Jane. "All About Cat Shows." Pets 101: Cats, Animal Planet, http://animal.discovery.com/pets/cat-show1.htm (Accessed May 2013).

"Pet Resources - Cat Glossary," Best Friends Pet Care, http://www.bestfriendspetcare.com/pet-resources/cat-glossary/ (Accessed May 2013).

"Plants and Your Cat," The Cat Fancier's Association, http://www.cfa.org/CatCare/HouseholdHazards/ToxicPlants.aspx (Accessed April 2013).
"Russian Blue," The Cat Fanciers' Association, http://cfa.org/Breeds/BreedsKthruR/RussianBlue.aspx (Accessed March 2013).

"Russian Blue," The International Cat Association, http://www.tica.org/public/breeds/rb/intro.php (Accessed June 2013).

"Russian Blue Cats," Cat Time, http://cattime.com/cat-breeds/russian-blue (Accessed March 2013).

Soden, Blair. "Cats Primped and Fluffed for 'Best of Best.'" ABC News. Oct. 14, 2007. http://abcnews.go.com/Entertainment/story?id=3729250&page=1 (Accessed May 2013).

Spadafori, Gina and Paul D. Pion, DVM, DAVCIM. Cats for Dummies, 2nd Ed. Hoboken, NJ: Wiley Publishing, Inc., 2000. Kindle Edition.

"The Temperament of the Russian Blue," Cats In Blue, http://www.cats-in-blue.dk/Russian%20Blue_e.htm (Accessed April 2013).

"Top Hypoallergenic Cat Breeds for People with Allergies," Catster, http://www.catster.com/cat-breeds/hypoallergenic-cat-breeds (Accessed May 2013).

"What Cats Hear," The Way of Cats Blog, http://www.wayofcats.com/blog/what-cats-hear/17870 (Accessed May 2013).

6

Frequently Asked Questions About Russian Blues

For detailed information on buying, keeping, and loving a Russian Blue cat, you'll need to read this book from the beginning. Here are some of the most frequently asked questions about this beautiful cat with its engaging green eyes and thoroughly wonderful personality.

Do Russian Blue cats really come from Russia?

Yes. These cats are believed to have originated in the Baltic Sea port of Archangel.

They began to appear in England in the 1800s, and the first Russian Blues were imported to the United States in the 1940s.

Are all gray cats Russian Blues?

No. Russian Blues are a distinct breed known for their dense double coats and vivid green eyes as well as for their engaging personalities. Other breeds often mistaken for Russian Blues include British Blues, Korats, the French Chartreux, and even gray domestic shorthairs that lack a pedigree of any kind.

Are Russian Blues loving, outgoing cats?

Yes and no. Russian Blues are very reserved around strangers, and may just disappear when someone "different" is in the house. They love their families very much and display open affection for their humans, but typically a Russian Blue will single out one person to whom they are totally devoted.
How do they get along with children?

They do best with well-mannered children, although they are tolerant with younger kids, seeming to realize that there's no intent to harm in the child's actions. Basically, when a Russian Blue has had enough, they just "evaporate."

These cats are very, very good at hiding and making themselves all but invisible. It's essential that children be taught to handle any animals — cats, dogs, or any other domestic species — gently and with respect.

Do Russian Blues tolerate other cats? What about dogs?

Russian Blues on a whole react entirely based on their experience of their surroundings.

They get along well with other pets, including dogs, that are willing to get along with them! Handle all introductions calmly and with supervision, and let the animals work it out for themselves.

You can't force any two cats or a cat and a dog to be best friends, but they will certainly determine their own boundaries and tolerances and work within them.

Which has the better disposition, a male or female Russian Blue?

The vast majority of Russian Blue cats sold to be pets have been neutered, which takes away many of the concerns about gender and personality.

Your best option is always to go with the kitten with which you seem to have an instant connection.

If, however, you are thinking about breeding your Russian Blue, you need to discuss personality with the breeder from whom you're buying the cat.

For the most part, however, there really is no difference in the nature of males and females. Both are gentle and affectionate.

Are Russian Blues good show cats?

Yes and no. Obviously this is a beautiful breed, but they don't like being around strangers and, although not aggressive or difficult in nature, they can be quite stubborn when they don't want to do something.

The decision to show a Russian Blue has to be made based on an individual's personality. In show circles, Russian Blues do have a reputation for being one of the more challenging breeds to exhibit.

Is shedding a major problem with this breed?

Shedding is a seasonal phenomenon with all cats, and is typically the heaviest in the spring when the animal is getting rid of its heavier, winter coat. Although Russian Blues have a wonderful, thick coat, they do not shed as much as other breeds, especially if they are receiving a well-balanced diet.

Why are they called blue? They look gray to me.

"Blue" is a show term among cat fanciers for just what you see — a gray cat. But Russian Blues are certainly not "plain" gray cats. In certain lights, their coats should shimmer with silver highlights giving them an unusually rich dimensionality.

What color eyes should a Russian Blue have?

All Russian Blue cats have vivid, intense green eyes with an alert and open expression. No other eye color is accepted in an adult cat. If a Russian Blue has yellow eyes, it would be classified as a "pet quality" cat and would not be eligible for breeding stock or as a show cat.

Breeders always require that cats with "faults" be spayed or neutered to prevent those traits from being passed on and diluting the quality of the breed.

Should a Russian Blue have any stripes in its coat?

Not as an adult. Some Russian Blue kittens are born with ghost stripes, usually on their tails, but those marks should fade as the cat ages.

All cats have a tabby gene, so stripes are possible, but in an adult, any stripes (or patches of different colored fur) will disqualify a Russian Blue for breeding or show purposes.

What is the life span of a Russian Blue and are they healthy cats?

The average life span for the breed is 15-20 years. They are hardy cats. They are not prone to sickness, and they have no specific genetic problems.

With regular and proper veterinarian care, your Russian Blue will be with you as a loving companion for many years.

Are Russian Blues intelligent?

There is very little that escapes the attention of a Russian Blue, so much so that some breeders say they can be difficult cats in the show ring, especially if they don't want the judge to handle them. Once they're out of the situation they don't like, they go right back to their loving, agreeable selves.

As pets, they're highly entertaining problem solvers, and excellent companions. If there's any "training" to be done, it's much more likely that your Russian Blue will be instructing you and not the other way around.

Also, these cats are extremely observant. They will remember where you put something and look for it months afterwards. Owners say that if you hide a special toy in a drawer, the cat will know it's there and ask for it. This is called "object permanence." Even though the cat cannot see the toy, they still understand that it exists inside the drawer. This is a sign of both good memory and intelligence.

Are Russian Blues needy?

A Russian Blue always singles out one person as their human of choice. They will want love and attention from that person and if they don't get it, they do have the capacity to be a little pesky.

A Russian Blue will do fine as a solo cat, but they don't like to be part of a large crowd where they can begin to feel neglected.

It's usually best not to keep them in big multi-cat households, although they will do very well with a feline buddy, especially another Russian Blue.

How will a Russian Blue get along while I'm at work?

Generally Russian Blues are just fine on their own for short periods of time, especially if they have a friend. At the end of the day, however, they'll be at the door waiting for you. These cats have a very good memory and they will learn your schedule quickly and expect you to keep to it!

7

Appendix 1 – Summary of Estimated Russian Blue Costs

Russian Blue Cat

Pet Quality
$400 (£264.55 / €305.50) - $700 (£462.96 / €534.63)

Show Quality
$800 (£529.10 / €611.01) - $2000 (£1322.75 / €1527.52).

Initial Set-Up

Food Bowls
$5.95 (£3.82 - €4.49)

or

Anti-whisker stress food bowls
$25 to $30 (£16.42 - £19.70 / €19.09 - €22.90)

Water Bowls
Stainless Steel - $9.99 (£6.42 / €7.55)

or

Circulating Water Fountain
 $30 (£19.70 / €22.90)

FOOD

Canned Cat Food (24 cans) (3 ounces / 85 grams per can) $21.64
(£13.91 / €16.36).

Dry Cat Food 16 lbs. (7.25 kg) $24.25 (£15.59 / €18.33).

LITTER BOXES

Litter box
(Covered) - $20 (£12.86 / €15.12)
(Uncovered) - $8.99 (£5.78 / €6.79)

Litter
(Clumping) – 28 lbs. (12.70 kg) - $16.99 (£10.93 / €12.84)
(Non-Clumping) – 10 lbs. (4.53 kg) - $6.28(£4.04 / €4.74)

GROOMING ACCESSORIES

Cat Brush $6.95 / £4.45 / €5.24

Wire Comb $10.75 / £6.88 / €8.11.

WINDOW PERCHES

Commercial perches that combine a bed with a platform and bracing supports cost about $30 (£19.70 / €22.91).

SCRATCHING POSTS

Elaborate cat "trees" range from $100 (£65 / €76.38) to $300 (£196.96 / €229.14) and more.

or

A simple carpeted pole with a single perch could cost as little as $30 (£19.70 / €22.91)

Anti-Scratching Products (to protect furniture)
Herbal sprays like pennyroyal or orange essence ($12-$15 / £7.87-£9.84 / €9.16-€11.45)

Double-sided tape products ($8-$10 / £5.25-£6.56 / €6.11-€7.63)

CRATES

Travel crate should cost from $30-$50 (£19.24-£32.07 / €22.66-€37.77)

TOY PRICES

Toy prices vary from a multi-pack of catnip mice $5-$7 (£3.28-£4.59 / €3.81-€5.34) to automated laser toy costing $27.99 / £17.93 / €21.13.

Russian Blues love toys, and you will need to change the items out as they become worn or soiled, or as the cat grows bored.

Initial toy purchase: $75 - $100
(£48.27 - £64.36 / €56.72 - €75.63)

Replacement as needed $15 - $25
(£9.65 - £16.09 / €11.34 - €18.90)
(Generally every 2-3 months.)

SPAYING AND NEUTERING

Spaying / neutering - $50 (£32.82 / €38.19),

VACCINATIONS

Individual shots are approximately $40 each (£25.74 / €30.25)
Distemper combination – 14 initial shots $560 (£360.44 / €423.55)

Feline Leukemia – 2 initial shots $80 (£51.49 / €60.50)
Rabies – 1 initial shot $40 each (£25.74 / €30.25)

PREVENTIVE DENTAL CARE

Oral hygiene kits
$7-$10 (£4.60-£6.56 / €5.34-€7.63)

ROUTINE VETERINARIAN VISITS

Office Visit $50 - $75 (£32.15 - £48.22 / €37.79 - €56.69)

ESTIMATED MONTHLY, YEARLY, LIFETIME COSTS

Estimated monthly cost: $130 (£85.40 / €99.28) a month

Estimated yearly cost: $1,565 (£1,028 / €1195.28)

Lifetime: $23,475 (£15,421.76 / €17,929.34) to $31,300 (£20,562.34 / €23,902.2

(Based on a life span of 15-20 years)

8

Appendix 2 –Naming your Russian Blue

Your Russian Blue kitten may come with a registered name, and many owners simply use a shortened version for the cat's every day name. But, if you go with the wisdom of T.S. Eliot in his poem, "The Naming of Cats," your work has barely begun there:

"The Naming of Cats is a difficult matter,
It isn't just one of your holiday games;
You may think at first I'm as mad as a hatter
When I tell you, a cat must have Three Different Names."

According to Eliot, there's always the name to which we mere humans are not privy:

"But above and beyond there's still one name left over,
And that is the name that you never will guess;
The name that no human research can discover--
But the cat himself knows, and will never confess."

Even if the cat is keeping mum on the subject, these beguiling little creatures frequently do name themselves, we just have to catch on and catch up to what they're trying to tell us. In the meantime, the owners of Russian Blues often play on the color of their cats:

- pewter, silver, slate, steel, ash, azure, aqua, cerulean, indigo, powder, periwinkle, sky

Or they go with something "Russian." There's a list of male and female Russian names below, and don't hesitate to have fun, "felinizing" any one to your heart's content.

A word to the wise, however, it's not so much that cats ignore us when we speak as that they can't hear low tones. Many men's voices are pitched too low for the cat to make out more than an indistinct mumble. This might explain why they so often appear to be ignoring men.

If you want your cat to actually respond to his name, make sure it has distinctive sounds that can be emphasized to get the cat's attention. Also, use hand signals when you speak your cat's name.

Most felines respond much better to non-verbal commands since all cats are astute observers of the world around them and communicate with one another through an intricate system of body language.

MALE NAMES

Alexei
Anatoly
Alexander
Andrei
Afanasy
Boris
Vladimir
Grigory
Dmitry
Zakhar
Ivan
Konstantin
Maxim or Meowskin
Mikhail
Nikita
Nikolay
Oleg
Pavel or Pawvel
Pyotr (Peter)
Roman
Sergei
Stanislav
Stepan
Valentin
Taras
Yury
Pushkin or Pusskin

FEMALE NAMES

Anna

Natalya

Camilla or Catilla

Tatyana - or Catyana

Katia or Catia

Olga

Veronica

Alena

Luisa

Karina

Svetlana

Natasha

Alina

Antonina

Victoriya

Darya

Valentina

Anastasia

Elena

Zoya

Eva

Yelena

Ekaterina or ECaterina

Zoe

Irina

Marta

Xenia

MALE AND FEMALE NAMES WITH ROYAL ASSOCIATIONS

Adela

Adelaide

Alexander

Alexandria

Augusta

Aymeric

Beatrice

Bourbon

Caroline

Chamberlain

Charles

Charlotte

Christinia

Constantine

Elizabeth

Eugenia

Fahd

Felipe

Frederica

Gustave

Hakon

Helena

Igor

Joachim

Kalani

Kenward

Kira

Kynaston

Ladislas

Lenchen

Leopold

Louisa

Magnus

Nicolas

Overon

Philip

Prince

Severn

Sofia

Sonja

Stuart

Tatiana

Titus

Valdemar

Victoria

Wilhelmina

Windsor

Xenia

York

Zara

9

Appendix 3 – Plants That Are Toxic to Cats

Source: The Cat Fancier's Association at www.cfa.org, http://www.cfa.org/CatCare/HouseholdHazards/ToxicPlants.aspx (Accessed May 2013).

Of the plants on this list, lilies are especially dangerous to cats. If you have any of these plants, they should be kept completely away from the cat. The cat should not be allowed into the area of the garden or yard where these plants are growing.

If your cat does eat any part of a poisonous plant, seek veterinary help for your pet immediately.

Almond (pits)
Aloe Vera
Alocasia
Amaryllis
Apple (seeds)
Apple Leaf Croto

Apricot (pits)

Arrowgrass

Asparagus Fern

Autumn Crocus

Avocado (fruit and pit)

Azalea Baby's Breath

Baneberry

Bayonet

Beargrass

Beech

Belladonna

Bird of Paradise

Bittersweet

Black-eyed Susan

Black Locust

Bleeding Heart

Bloodroot

Bluebonnet

Box

Boxwood

Branching Ivy

Buckeyes

Buddhist Pine

Burning Bush

Buttercup Cactus

Candelabra

Caladium

Calla Lily

Castor Bean

Ceriman

Charming Dieffenbachia

Cherry (pits, seeds, leaves)

Cherry Laurel

Chinaberry

Chinese Everegreen

Christmas Rose

Chrysanthemum

Cineria

Clematis

Cordatum

Coriaria

Cornflower

Corn Plant

Cornstalk Plant

Croton

Corydalis

Crocus, Autumn

Crown of Thorns

Cuban Laurel

Cutleaf Philodendron

Cycads

Cyclamen

Daffodil

Daphne

Datura

Deadly Nightshade

Death Camas

Devil's Ivy

Delphinium

Decentrea

Dieffenbachia

Dracaena Palm

Dragon Tree

Dumb Cane

Easter Lily

Eggplant

Elaine

Elderberry

Elephant Ear

Emerald Feather

English Ivy

Eucalyptus

Euonymus

Evergreen Ferns

Fiddle-leaf Fig

Florida Beauty

Flax

Four O'Clock

Foxglove

Fruit Salad Plant

Geranium

German Ivy

Giant Dumb Cane

Glacier Ivy

Golden Chain

Gold Dieffenbachia

Gold Dust Dracaena

Golden Glow

Golden Pothos

Gopher Purge

Hahn's Self-Branching Ivy

Heartland Philodendron

Hellebore

Hemlock, Poison

Hemlock, Water

Henbane

Holly

Horsebeans

Horsebrush

Hellebore

Horse Chestnuts

Hurricane Plant

Hyacinth

Hydrangea

Indian Rubber Plant

Indian Tobacco

Iris

Iris Ivy

Jack in the Pulpit

Janet Craig Dracaena

Japanese Show Lily

Java Beans

Jessamine

Jerusalem Cherry

Jimson Weed

Jonquil

Jungle Trumpets

Kalanchoe

Lacy Tree Philodendron

Lantana

Larkspur

Laurel

Lily

Lily Spider

Lily of the Valley

Locoweed

Lupine

Madagascar Dragon Tree

Marble Queen
Marigold
Marijuana
Mescal Bean
Mexican Breadfruit
Miniature Croton
Mistletoe
Mock Orange
Monkshood
Moonseed
Morning Glory
Mother-in-Law's Tongue
Morning Glory
Mountain Laurel
Mushrooms
Narcissus
Needlepoint Ivy
Nephytis
Nightshade Oleander
Onion
Oriental Lily
Peace Lily
Peach (pits and leaves)
Pencil Cactus
Peony
Periwinkle
Philodendron
Pimpernel
Plumosa Fern
Poinciana
Poinsettia (low toxicity)
Poison Hemlock

Poison Ivy

Poison Oak

Pokeweed

Poppy

Potato

Pothos

Precatory Bean

Primrose

Privet, Common

Red Emerald

Red Princess

Red-Margined Dracaena

Rhododendron

Rhubarb

Ribbon Plan

Rosemary Pea

Rubber Plant

Saddle Leaf Philodendron

Sago Palm

Satin Pathos

Schefflera

Scotch Broom

Silver Pothos

Skunk Cabbage

Snowdrops

Snow on the Mountain

Spotted Dumb Cane

Staggerweed

Star of Bethlehem

String of Pearls

Striped Dracaena

Sweetheart Ivy

Sweetpea

Swiss Cheese plant

Tansy Mustard

Taro Vine

Tiger Lily

Tobacco

Tomato Plant (green fruit, stem, leaves)

Tree Philodendron

Tropic Snow Dieffenbachia

Tulip

Tung Tree

Virginia Creeper

Water Hemlock

Weeping Fig

Wild Call

Wisteria Yews

English Yew

Western Yew

American Yew

[10]

Relevant Websites

GENERAL INFORMATION

Breed Profile: Getting to Know the Russian Blue at
http://www.catscenterstage.com/breeds/russian-blue2.shtml

CFA Russian Blue Breed Council at http://russianbluebc.org/

CFA Russian Blue Breed Profile at
http://www.cfa.org/Breeds/BreedsKthruR/RussianBlue.aspx

Russian Blue Fanciers at http://www.russianblue.info/

The Temperament of the Russian Blue at http://www.cats-in-blue.dk/Russian%20Blue_e.htm

CAT SHOWS

Cat Shows in the U.S. at http://www.catshows.us

Cat Fanciers' Federation Show Page at
http://www.cffinc.org/pages/show-page.php

The International Cat Association Official Show Calendar at
http://ticamembers.org/calendar/

BREEDER DIRECTORIES

Cats and Kittens at http://www.catsandkittens.com
Cat Channel at http://www.catchannel.com/classifieds/listing-russian-blue.aspx

Cat Fanciers' Association Inc. Registry of Pedigreed Cats at
http://secure.cfa.org/Search.aspx
Fanciers Breeder Referral List at http://www.breedlist.com/

BREEDERS BY COUNTRY

Note, this is by no means a complete list. Use the breeder directories or your Internet search engine of choice to locate additional catteries.

See Chapter 2 - Welcoming a Russian Blue Into Your Home for more information on working with breeders to acquire a cat or kitten.

AUSTRALIA

Samnicki Russian Blues www.samnickirussianblues.com.au

Siblu Russians at www.siblurussians.com

Raska Cattery at www.russianblue.com.au

Tintola at www.russianblue.com.au

Tyana Russians at www.tyanakirashan.com

Keehotay Russian Blues at www.keehotayrussians.com

Barishka Russian Blues at www.barishka.com

Kimara at www.kimara.iinet.net.au

Blebebob at www.bluebebop.webs.com

AUSTRIA

A Flashpaws Russian Blue at www.flashpaws.net

Tolstoi's Child at www.tolstoischild.russianblue.at

BELGIUM

Cattery Blue Angels at www.blueangels.be

Cattery Benjoblana at www.benjoblana.be

Cattery Casimir at www.catterycasimir.be

DENMARK

Alba Blue at www.albablue.net

Basis Cats at www.basiscat.dk

Hesseldal Russian Blue at www.cats-in-blue.dk

Paragon Blue at www.paragonblue.dk

Tanisjka's Russian Blue at www.tanisjka.dk

FINLAND

Fin*Zarin at www.zarin.net

Starstrucks at www.starstrucks.net

Fin*Harmuan at www.harmuan.net

Kaizahre at www.kaizahre.net

Meadowpaws at www.meadowpaws.net

GERMANY

Jumillas Russian Blue at www.jumillas.com

Anarrimas Russian Blue at www.anarrimas-russisch-blau.de
(our both cats are from Anarrimas)

Tyuda's Russian Blue at www.tyuda.de

ZarenSilber at www.russischblau-katzen.de

Cheeky Rascal at www.cheeky-rascal.de

Kamenko at www.kamenko.de

RUSSIA

Ever Blue at http://www.elladacats.ru/ (Note this site is in Russian.)

UNITED STATES

Catera Cattery at http://www.cateracattery.com/

Emjoy's Russian Blue Cattery at
http://www.kathrynsgallery.com/emjoyscattery/home.html

Ever Blue at http://www.elladacats.ru/ (Note this site is in Russian.)

Izmaylovo Park Russian Cats at http://www.therussianblue.com/

Platina Luna at http://platinaluna.com/

Prairie Home Cattery at http://prairiehome.tripod.com/

Rubanthom Cattery at http://www.rubanthom.com/

Snow Island Russian Blues at http://snow-island.russianblue.net/

Tylona Cattery at http://www.tylona.com/

Wynterwynd at http://www.wynterwynd.com/

Glossary

Ailurophile - A person who loves cats.

Ailurophobe - A person who fears or even hates cats.

Allergen - In relation to cats, the primary allergen, the substance that causes an allergic reaction in some people, is Fel d 1, a protein produced by the cat's sebaceous glands, and present in its saliva.

Allergy - A high level of sensitivity present in some people to a given substance, like the protein Fel d 1 in cats. Generally the reaction includes, but is not limited to, watering eyes, sneezing, itching, and skin rashes.

Alter - A term which refers to the neutering or spaying of a cat or dog.

Animal Shelter - Any organization that exists for the purpose of caring for and arranging adoptions for homeless pets.

Bloodline - The verifiable line of descent that establishes an animals' pedigree.

Blue - The accepted term for feline coat colors that range in tone from a bluish gray to a lighter slate gray.

Breed Standard - A set of standards for a given breed formulated by parent breed clubs and used as the basis for evaluating show quality animals.

Breed - Term that refers to a group of cats with defined physical characteristics that are related by common ancestry.

Breeder - A person who works with a particular breed of cats, producing offspring from high-quality dams and sires for the purpose of maintaining and improving the genetic quality of the line.

Breeding - The process in which dams and sires are paired for the purpose of producing offspring.

Breeding Program - An organized and ongoing program in which cats are mated selectively to produce offspring that are ideal examples of the breed.

Breeding Quality - A term describing a cat that meets the standards of a given breed to a degree sufficient to be included in a breeding program.

Breed True - The phrase which describes the capacity of a male and female cat to produce kittens that closely resemble themselves in accepted elements of the breed standard.

Carpal Pads - Located on a cat's front legs at the "wrists," these pads provide added traction for the animal's gait.

Castrate - The medical procedure whereby a male cat's testicles are removed.

Caterwaul - A feline vocalization that produces a discordant, shrill sound.

Cat Fancy - Term used to describe the overall group of registered associations clubs, and individuals that breed and show cats.

Catnip - A member of the mint family, this aromatic perennial herb (Nepeta cataria) contains an oil to which some cats are strongly attracted and to which they respond with a kind of "stoned" intoxication. Kittens cannot respond to catnip until they are 8-9 months of age.

Cattery - Any establishment that exists for the purpose of housing cats, and where they are bred as part of an organized program.

Certified Pedigree - A pedigree that has been issued in an official capacity by a feline registering association.

Clowder - A collective term for a group of cats.

Coat - Term referring to a cat's fur.

Crate - Container used to safely transport cats from one location to another or to confine them temporarily for their own safety.

Crepuscular - Although known in popular lore as nocturnal animals, cats are actually crepuscular, meaning they are most active at dusk and dawn.

Crossbred - A cat that is the product of breeding a sire and a dam of different breeds.

Dam -The female in a parenting set of cats.

Dander - The small scales of hair and skin that are shed by an animal. Often responsible for allergic reactions in individuals with a sensitivity to the substance.

Declawing - A highly controversial surgical procedure that removes a cat's claws permanently.

Desex - Describes the alteration of an animal by neutering or spaying.

Domesticated - Animals that have been tamed to live with or work with humans, or that have chosen to cultivate such a relationship.

Ear Mites - Microscopic parasites that feed on the lining of a cat's ear canal, causing debris to build up, generating a foul odor, and resulting in extreme itching.

Entire - A term describing a cat that has an intact reproductive system.

Exhibitor - An individual that participates in organized cat shows.

Fel d 1 - A protein produced by the cat's sebaceous glands, and present in its saliva, which causes an allergic reaction in some people. Feline - A member of the family Felidae. Includes lions, tigers, jaguars, and wild and domestic cats.

Fleas - Various bloodsucking insects of the order Siphonaptera. They are wingless, and their legs are adapted for jumping. They are parasitical, and feed off warm-blooded animals.

Flehmening/ Flehmen Reaction - A facial gesture in cats that is often mistaken for a grimace. In reality, the cat is drawing in air to pass it over a special structure in the roof of the mouth called the Jacobsen's Organ, which functions as a second set of nostrils and allows cats to "taste" a scent.

Gene pool - In a population of organisms, the "gene pool" is the collective genetic information relative to reproduction.

Genes - Determine particular characteristics in a given organism. They are a distinct hereditary unit and consist of a DNA sequence occupying a specific location on a chromosome.

Genetic - Refers to any trait, characteristic, tendency, or condition that is inherited.

Genetically Linked Defects - Health specific problems or those relative to temperament that are passed from one generation to the next.

Genetics - The scientific study of heredity.

Genotype - Refers to the genetic makeup of an organism or a group of organisms.

Groom - The act of caring for the coat of a feline, which may include brushing, combing, trimming, or washing.

Guard Hair - Long, coarse hairs that form the outer layer of a cat's coat.

Heat - The seasonal estrus cycle of a female cat (or any other mammal).

Hereditary - Any characteristic, trait, disease, or condition that can be genetically transmitted from parent to offspring.

Histamine - A physiologically active amine in plant and animal tissue released from mast cells as part of an allergic reaction in humans.

Hock - Anatomical term describing the ankle of a cat's hind leg.

Household Pet - A cat not registered to be exhibited or shown in competition.

Housetraining - The process whereby a cat is trained to use a litter box to live cleanly in a house.

Humane Societies - Any one of a number of groups that work to put an end to animal suffering due to overt acts of cruelty and other impoverishing or harmful circumstances.

Immunization - The use of inoculations to create immunity against disease. Also referred to as vaccination.

Innate - A quality, trait, or tendency present at birth and thus inborn

Inbreeding - When two closely-related cats of the same breed are mated.

Instinct - A pattern of behavior in a species that is inborn and comes in response to specific environmental stimuli.

Intact - Animals that are intact possess their complete reproductive system. They have not been neutered or spayed.

Jacobsen's Organ - An organ located in the roof of a cat's mouth that allows it to "taste" a scent. Appears as two small openings and is regarded as a second set of "nostrils."

Kindle - A collective term for a group of kittens. An alternate term is "chowder."

Kitten - Young cats under the age of 6 months.

Lactation - Process by which the mammary glands form and secrete milk.

Lactating - Term used for a mammalian mother when she is secreting or producing milk.

Litter - The number of offspring in a single birth. Generally 3-4 in cats, although 6-10 is not uncommon.

Litter Box - A container filled with commercial kitty litter or sand and used in the home as a sanitary and manageable location for a cat to urinate and defecate.

Longhair - Cats with varying lengths of long hair, typically with plumed tails and prominent neck ruffs.

Mites - Small arachnids (of the order Acarina) that are parasites on animals and plants. Often seen in the ears of felines.

Moggy - The term for a mixed breed cat in the United Kingdom.

Muzzle - In cats, the part of the head projecting forward including the mouth, nose, and jaws. May also be referred to as the snout.

Neuter - The term used to describe castrating a male cat.

Nictitating Membrane - A cat's third eyelid, which is a transparent inner eyelid that serves to protect and moisten the eye.

Nocturnal - Term used to describe animals that are most active at night. It is mistakenly applied to cats, who are actually crepuscular, being most active at dawn and dusk.

Obligate Carnivore – In relation to cats, this term describes their biological need to consume meat.

Odd-Eyed - **Eyes** of two different colors presenting in a single individual.

Papers - The documentation of a cat's pedigree and registration.

Pedigree - A cat's genealogy presented in writing and spanning three or more generations.

Pet Quality - A cat that does not sufficiently meet the accepted standard for its breed to be shown in competition or to be used in a breeding program.

Queen - An intact female cat, one that has not been spayed.

Quick - The vascular portion of a cat's claw that will, if clipped, bleed profusely.

Rabies - A viral disease that is highly infectious and typically fatal to warm-blooded animals. It attacks the central nervous system and is transmitted by the bite of an infected animal.

Recognition - The point at which a cat breed is officially accepted under a cat fancy organization's rules.

Registered Cat - A cat registered through a recognized feline association that has documentation of its ancestry.

Registered Name - The official name used by a registered cat, which is typically long and reflective of its ancestry.

Registration - The record of the particulars of a cat's birth and ancestry filed with an official organization.

Scratching Post - A tower-like structure covered in carpet or rope that allows a cat to sharpen and clean its claws inside the house without being destructive to furniture.

Secondary Coat - In a cat, the fine hairs of the undercoat.

Semi-Longhair - Long-haired cats with a medium-length coat.

Shelter - Any local organization that exists for the purpose of rescuing and caring for homeless and stray animals. Also works to find permanent homes for these animals.

Show - An organized exhibition in which judges evaluate cats according to accepted standards for each breed and make awards accordingly.

Show Cat - Cats that participate in shows.

Show Quality - Cats that meet the standards for their breed at a sufficient level to compete in organized cat shows.

Show Standard - A description of the ideal qualities of a breed of cats used as the basis for which the cats are judged in competition. Also known as standard of point.

Silver - A term used to describe a light shading of gray. Often seen as a tipping on darker fur, as is the case with the Russian Blue.

Sire - The male member of a parenting set of cats.

Spay - The surgery to remove a female cat's ovaries.

Spray - A territorial behavior typically seen in male cats whereby the animal emits a stream of urine as a marker.

Stud - An intact male cat that has not been altered and is used as part of a breeding program.

Subcutaneous - Placed just below the skin, as in an injection.

Tapetum Lucidum - The interior portion of a cat's eye that aids in night vision and is highly reflective.

Undercoat - The layer of a cat's coat that is composed of down hairs.

Undercolor - The color of the hair lying closest to a cat's skin.

Vaccine - A weakened or dead preparation of a bacterium, virus, or other pathogen used to stimulate the production of antibodies for the purpose of creating immunity against the disease when injected.

Vibrissae – The scientific name for a cat's whiskers, which function as tactile sensing organs.

Wean - The point at which a kitten begins to eat solid food and is taken off its mother's milk as the primary source of nutrition.

Whisker Break - Refers to an indentation of the upper jaw on a cat.

Whisker Pad - The thickened or fatty pads on either side of a cat's face holding rows of sensory whiskers.

Whole - A cat of either gender that is intact, and has not been neutered or spayed.

For more information and a weblog, visit:

www.russian-blue-cats.com – the official website

Index

Printed in Great Britain
by Amazon

59656041R00078